Vegetarian Cookbook

70 Easy Veggie Recipes For Classic And Modern Food From Thailand

---

Emma Yang

© **Copyright 2021 by (Emma Yang) - All rights reserved**.

This document is geared towards providing exact and reliable information in regards to the topic and issue covered. The publication is sold with the idea that the publisher is not required to render accounting, officially permitted, or otherwise, qualified services. If advice is necessary, legal or professional, a practiced individual in the profession should be ordered.

- From a Declaration of Principles which was accepted and approved equally by a Committee of the American Bar Association and a Committee of
Publishers and Associations.

In no way is it legal to reproduce, duplicate, or transmit any part of this document in either electronic means or in printed format. Recording of this publication is strictly prohibited and any storage of this document is not allowed unless with written permission from the publisher. All rights reserved.

The information provided herein is stated to be truthful and consistent, in that any liability, in terms of inattention or otherwise, by any usage or abuse of any policies, processes, or directions contained within is the solitary and utter responsibility of the recipient reader. Under no circumstances will any legal responsibility or blame be held against the publisher for any reparation, damages, or monetary loss due to the information herein, either directly or indirectly.

Respective authors own all copyrights not held by the publisher.
The information herein is offered for informational purposes solely, and is universal as so. The presentation of the information is without contract or any type of guarantee assurance.

The trademarks that are used are without any consent, and the publication of the trademark is without permission or backing by the trademark owner. All trademarks and brands within this book are for clarifying purposes only and are the owned by the owners themselves, not affiliated with this document.

Contents

INTRODUCTION 7

CHAPTER 1: TRADITIONAL THAI BREAKFAST RECIPES 8

1.1: Jok (Rice Porridge) 8

1.2: Khao Tom (Rice Soup) 9

1.3: Kai Jeow (Thai-Style Omelet) 10

1.4: Pa Thong Ko (Thai doughnuts) 11

1.5: Kanom Krok (Small Coconut Pancakes) 12

1.6: Thai Vegetable Omelet 13

1.7: Thai Tea Overnight Oats Recipe 14

1.8: Thai Peanut Overnight Oats 15

1.9: Yam Kai (Thai Eggs) With Leftover Grains 16

1.10: Thai Scrambled Eggs 17

CHAPTER 2: DELICIOUS AND EASY LUNCH TIME RECIPES 18

2.1: Chickpea and Vegetable Coconut Curry 18

2.2: Thai Peanut Coconut Cauliflower Chickpea Curry 19

2.3: Stir-Fried Courgettes and Egg Recipe 20

2.4: Bangkok Coconut Curry Noodle Bowls 21

2.5: Healing Lemongrass Chickpea Thai Green Curry 23

2.6: Creamy Thai Sweet Potato Curry 24

2.7: Red Curry with Vegetables 25

2.8: Thai Red Curry with Asparagus and Tofu 26

2.9: Green Curry Noodle Soup 28

2.10: Easy Thai Curry Hot Pot 29

2.11: Thai Yellow Curry with Chickpeas and Cauliflower 31

2.12: Real Veggie Pad Thai (Vegan/Gluten-Free) 33

2.13: Thai Green Vegetable Curry 34

2.14: Thai Chilli Broccoli Salad Recipe 35

2.15: Thai Pomelo Salad Recipe 36

2.16: Roasted Thai Yellow Curry Potatoes 37

2.17: Smashed Potatoes with Thai-Style Chile and Herb Sauce 38

CHAPTER 3: QUICK AND EASY DINNER RECIPES 40

3.1: Spaghetti Squash Pad Thai 40

3.2: Steamed Dumplings with Shiitake Mushrooms, Ginger, and Coriander 42

3.3: Thai Pumpkin Curry (Vegan/Gluten-Free) 44

3.4: Authentic Thai Tofu Satay (Vegetarian/Vegan) 45

3.5: Thai Stir-Fried Noodles with Vegetables 47

3.6: Easy Thai Rice Noodles with Basil 48

3.7: Thai Heavenly Pineapple Fried Rice 50

3.8: Easy Thai Coconut Rice 51

3.9: Thai Yellow Rice 52

3.10: Easy Stir-Fried Eggplant 53

3.11: Vegetarian Thai Tom Yum Soup 55

3.12: Vegetable Noodle Soup with Tofu & Lemongrass (Vegan/Gluten-Free) 56

3.13: Thai Pumpkin Coconut Soup 57

3.14: Stir-Fried Greens 58

3.15: Thai Stir-Fried Spinach with Garlic and Peanuts 59

3.16: Thai Soyabean in Cabbage Cups Recipe 60

3.17: Thai-Style Baked Seasoned Sweet Potatoes and Purple Yams 61

CHAPTER 4: MOUTHWATERING DESSERTS RECIPES 63

4.1: Thai Mango Sticky Rice Dessert 63

4.2: Musician's Dessert 64

4.3: Avocado Cream Dessert 64

4.4: Thai Dessert Rice Cups 65

4.5: Mini Pudding in Sweet Coconut Sauce 66

4.6: Thai- style Pineapple Fritter 67

4.7: Thai mango ice cream 68

4.8: Thai Banana-Lychee Dessert in Coconut Milk 69

4.9: Star Fruit in Mango-Orange Sauce 70

4.10: Thai Sweet Chili and Caramel Topping 71

4.11: Thai Bananas in Coconut Milk 72

4.12: Coconut Tapioca Pudding with Mango and Lime 73

4.13: Banana Spring Rolls 74

4.14: Thai Steamed Banana Cake 75

4.15: Shaved Ice Dessert - Thai Style 76

4.16: Easy Thai Fruit Salad 76

CHAPTER 5: THAI DRINKS RECIPES 78

5.1: Lychee-Thai Chili Lemonade Recipe 78

5.2: Tom Yum Coca-Cola 79

5.3: Pandan and Lemongrass Tea 80

5.4: Lychee Champagne Cocktail 80

5.5: Thai One On 81

5.6: Thai Basil Daiquiri Recipe 82

5.7: Thai Lemonade 82

5.8: Thai-Style Pina Colada 84

5.9: Thai Iced Tea Recipe 84

5.10: Thai Lemon Iced Tea 85

CONCLUSION..86

Introduction

Vegetables are an important component of Thai cuisine, and many delectable Thai dishes feature them as the main ingredient. Thai cuisine is balanced and nutritious because of the vegetables.

Thai people use a lot of green vegetables in their diets, which are a good source of basic nutrition and will reduce blood sugar levels, the reduction of obesity, maintenance of a healthy weight, and reduce cholesterol.

Furthermore, since Thai food uses many noodles, rice, and vegetables as a foundation, it is simple to make vegan dishes. Since there is no cheese, butter, or milk in the original recipe, and meat is just a small part of it, changing them would not significantly alter the flavor.

Thai cuisine necessitates the balancing of disparate elements to achieve a harmonious result, necessitating a great deal of attention to detail to achieve the right flavor balance and good presentation.

You can prepare Thai vegetarian recipes at home by learning various ingredients that you will need to start cooking. By reading this wonderful book, you will learn that there is no necessity to add meat to your meal when vegetarian Thai recipes already have wonderful flavor. This book contains over 70 different breakfast, lunch, dinner, desserts, and drinks recipes. You can easily begin cooking these Thai recipes at home, which are full of flavor and have balanced nutrition without the use of meat.

Chapter 1: Traditional Thai Breakfast Recipes

There are thousands of different Thai dishes, but only a few are called Thai breakfast only dishes, meaning they are only available for breakfast in the morning.

Instead, you can eat the same foods for breakfast, lunch, and dinner in Thailand.

All of the dishes mentioned below are nutritious and traditional Thai breakfast recipes.

1.1: Jok (Rice Porridge)

Preparation time: 5 minutes

Cooking time: 90 minutes

Serving: 1

Ingredients

- Rice: two cups (jasmine is used traditionally, but other types of rice are also fine)
- Vegan chicken stock or regular vegetable stock: three-four liters
- Suggested toppings:
- Crumbled tofu with soy sauce and garlic (fried)
- Sliced mushrooms with soy sauce and garlic (fried)
- Spring onions (sliced)
- Fresh ginger (matchsticks)
- Leafy greens (spinach, cabbage, or spring greens)
- Carrot (grated)

Instructions:

1. Bring 3 liters of stock to a boil in a pan –make it upright in the pan if using stock cubes/powder.
2. Rinse jasmine rice thoroughly until the water runs clear in a sieve.
3. Toss in the rice and carry to a low simmer.
4. With the lid on, cook for about 90 minutes.

5. Turn off the stove when the rice begins to break down and resembles a soupy porridge consistency.

6. Serve with a range of delicious toppings in a dish.

1.2: Khao Tom (Rice Soup)

Preparation time: 10 minutes

Cooking time: 10 minutes

Servings: 4

Ingredients

- Low sodium vegetable stock: 500 ml
- Shredded preserved turnip: two tablespoons
- Thai white/thin soy sauce: one tablespoon
- Thai seasoning sauce: one tablespoon
- Ground white pepper: ¼ teaspoon
- Cooked leftover jasmine rice: approximately one cup
- Tofu cubed: ¼ - ½ cup
- Chinese celery chopped: two-three tablespoons
- Spring onion sliced: one tablespoon
- Fresh coriander, roughly chopped: one tablespoon
- Crispy garlic, fried in oil: one tablespoon
- Vegan fish sauce mixed with sliced bird's eye chilies: personal taste
- Chilli vinegar: personal taste
- White sugar: personal taste
- Additional white pepper: personal taste

Instructions:

1. Add the salted radish, seasoning sauce, white pepper, soy sauce, and jasmine rice to the boiling stock.

2. Add the Chinese celery and tofu after five minutes of simmering.

3. Cook for an additional 2-3 minutes before spooning into a wide mixing bowl.

4. Garnish with fresh coriander, spring onion, and crispy garlic.

5. Serve hot with chili vinegar, white pepper, sugar and fish sauce (vegan), and fresh chilies to the season for your desired tastes.

1.3: Kai Jeow (Thai-Style Omelet)

Preparation time: 2 minutes

Cooking time: 3 minutes

Serving: 1

Ingredients

- Olive oil: one teaspoon
- Eggs: two
- Spring onion: one (thinly sliced)
- Soy sauce: half teaspoon
- Salt and pepper
- To serve:
- Sriracha hot sauce (optional)
- Coriander

Instructions

1. In a pan, heat the oil.
2. Combine the eggs, spring onion, soy sauce, salt, and pepper in a mixing bowl.
3. Pour the contents into the hot pan. Cook for 1-2 minutes, or until lightly browned, then flip and cook for another 1-2 minutes.
4. Drizzle with coriander sriracha sauce to taste and serve right away.

1.4: Pa Thong Ko (Thai doughnuts)

Preparation time: 35 minutes

Cooking time: 5-7 minutes

Serving: 10

Ingredients
- All-purpose flour: three cups
- Water: one cup
- Baking powder: one teaspoon
- Baking soda: ¼ teaspoon
- Sugar: one teaspoon
- Vegetable oil: one tablespoon

Instructions:

1. Combine the baking soda, baking powder, salt, and sugar in a mixing bowl. Add water and stir thoroughly. Stir in the all-purpose flour with a fork for a few seconds.

2. Mix in the vegetable oil until it is well mixed. Cover and set aside at room temperature for 4 hours.

3. In a deep pan, bring the oil to heat. Using flour, dust the work surface. Form a sausage out of the dough. Cut into 1" pieces, roll into a ball, then roll out into a thin circle (4-5mm) or cut into 2" pieces to create the other style. To make an X shape, dab a little water in the center of each piece and stick another piece to it.

4. Carefully drop doughnuts, two at a time, into hot oil and fry until golden.

1.5: Kanom Krok (Small Coconut Pancakes)

Preparation time: 10 minutes

Cooking time: 5 minutes

Servings: 20

Ingredients

- Coconut Milk: one cup
- Glutinous Rice flour: half cup
- Regular Rice Flour: half cup
- Sugar: one-two tablespoons
- Salt: to taste
- Oil: as needed
- Spring Onions
- Shredded coconut

Instructions

1. Combine the salt, sugar, and coconut milk in a large mixing bowl.
2. Mix in the rice flour thoroughly.
3. The batter should be a bit thin.
4. Now heat an appe pan and fill each hole with oil.
5. Cook for a few seconds after pouring in the batter. Cover with a layer of spring onion and coconut. Cook for another minute.
6. Serve and enjoy.

1.6: Thai Vegetable Omelet

Preparation time: 5 minutes

Cooking time: 5 minutes

Servings: 1

Ingredients
Thai dressing:
- Lime juice: half
- Fish sauce: half tablespoon
- Brown sugar: half tablespoon
- Chopped small chili: one
- Sweet chili sauce: 1 ½ tablespoon
- Rice vinegar: half tablespoon
- Peanut oil/olive oil: 1 teaspoon
- Water: 1 tablespoon
- Mix all together until combined.

Omelet:
- Olive oil
- Garlic
- Leftover veggies of choice (mushrooms, bok choy, snow peas, asparagus, bean sprouts, broccoli): about one cup
- Salt: to taste
- Eggs: two
- Water: two tablespoons
- Turmeric powder: a pinch

Instructions:

1. Stir-fry garlic, Mushrooms, Asparagus, Broccoli, Snow Peas, Bok Choy, and Bean Sprouts in a cast-iron skillet with a little oil. Keep cooking the vegetables until they are tender but still crisp, seasoning with salt and pepper. Remove from the stove and set aside.

2. Combine the eggs, water, salt, and turmeric in a medium mixing bowl.

3. In the cast-iron skillet, add a little oil and heat it. Then add the beaten eggs. Cook, occasionally stirring, until the eggs begin to set.

4. While the omelet continues to cook in the hot skillet, remove it from the heat, cover it with the cooked assorted vegetables, and fold the omelet over them.

5. Sprinkle the Thai dressing over the salad and serve the remaining dressing on the side.

1.7: Thai Tea Overnight Oats Recipe

Preparation time: 10 minutes

Cooking time: 0 minutes

Servings: 4-5

Ingredients

- Black tea bags: four (3 cups water)
- Cardamom: half teaspoon
- Star anise pods: two (optional)
- Turmeric: half teaspoon (optional, for color only)
- Coconut sugar: ¼ cup (plus more to taste)
- Full-fat coconut milk or coffee creamer: one cup
- Vanilla extract: half teaspoon (optional)
- Lime juice: half lime
- Quick-cooking or rolled oats: three cups
- Chia seeds: ¼ cup

Instructions

1. In a huge mixing bowl, combine the black tea bags, cardamom, and optional turmeric, and star anise.

2. Pour nearly boiling water over the tea and steep for 5 minutes before removing the tea bags.

3. Mix the coconut sugar into the tea. Blend in the coconut milk, lime juice, and vanilla extract until smooth liquid forms.

4. In a bowl, combine the oats and chia seeds and stir well. Allow 5 minutes for the mixture to thicken, then taste the oatmeal and adjust the sweetness as needed. Refrigerate the oatmeal for at least 4 hours, preferably overnight.

5. As required, garnish and serve.

1.8: Thai Peanut Overnight Oats

Preparation time: 10 minutes

Cooking time: 0 minutes

Servings: 1

Ingredients

- Rolled oats: half cup
- Unsweetened coconut milk beverage: half cup
- Natural peanut butter: 1 tablespoon
- Tamari: 1 teaspoon
- Curry powder: half teaspoon
- Cooked greens: ¼ cup (spinach or kale)
- Chopped tomatoes: two tablespoons
- Chopped cilantro: one tablespoon

Instructions:

1. Combine the oats, tamari, coconut milk, curry powder, and peanut butter in a bowl or cup. Refrigerate overnight, covered.
2. Before serving, garnish with greens, tomatoes, and cilantro.

1.9: Yam Kai (Thai Eggs) With Leftover Grains

Preparation time: 5 minutes

Cooking time: 10 minutes

Servings: 2

Ingredients

- Freshly squeezed lime juice: one and a half tablespoons (from half lime)
- Fish sauce: one and a half tablespoons
- Chile paste (sambal oelek): one and a half teaspoons
- Cooked barley, sorghum, quinoa, millet, or brown rice cooled: one cup/190 g
- Large eggs: four
- Vegetable oil: one tablespoon
- Shallots: four (thinly sliced)
- Scallions: four (green and white parts separated, cut in 2inch lengths)

Instructions:

1. Combine the lime juice, fish sauce, one teaspoon chile paste, and the cooked grain of your choice in a medium bowl and set aside.

2. In a small mixing cup, whisk together the eggs and the remaining half teaspoon of chile paste and set aside.

3. In a big heavy sauté pan, heat half tablespoon of oil over medium-high flame.

4. Add the shallots, the white sections of the scallions, and cook, occasionally stirring, until the shallots are very dark brown.

5. Cook for one minute with the scallion greens and the remaining half tablespoon of oil. Pour in the egg mixture and cook for 30 seconds without stirring, then turn and stir, breaking it up a little but holding good-size bits together, for about 45 seconds.

6. Pour in the grain mixture and cook for one minute, turning with a spatula until heated through.

7. Serve the food.

1.10: Thai Scrambled Eggs

Preparation time: 10 minutes

Cooking time: 10 minutes

Servings: 2

Ingredients

- Eggs: 4
- Coconut Milk Seasoning: five tablespoons (75ml)
- Butter: half oz (12g)
- Spring onions: three (sliced)
- Red chili: half (finely chopped and deseeded)
- Root ginger: one teaspoon (5ml) (peeled and grated)
- Ciabatta, sliced & extra spring onions: to serve (sliced)

Instructions:

1. Blend the eggs, coconut milk, salt, and pepper in a small mixing bowl.

2. In a small nonstick, melt the butter frying pan.

3. Stir in the spring onions, chilies, and ginger until all is well combined.

4. Pour the egg mixture in and set aside for 20 seconds without stirring. Using a wooden spoon, stir it from the bottom of the pan, raising and folding it over. Remove the eggs from the heat when they are gently set but still slightly runny in spots.

5. Toast the ciabatta slices, butter and layer scrambled eggs on top, garnishing with extra sliced spring onions.

Chapter 2: Delicious and Easy Lunch Time Recipes

Vegan Thai food is a simple way to add the flavors of Thailand to your home kitchen. Following are some traditional Thai recipes and flavors that are easily translatable into delicious vegan food cooked at home and are the best option for your lunchtime.

2.1: Chickpea and Vegetable Coconut Curry

Preparation time: 10 minutes

Cooking time: 20 minutes

Servings: 4

Ingredients:
- Extra-virgin olive oil: one tablespoon
- Red onion: one (thinly sliced)
- Red bell pepper: one (thinly sliced)
- Fresh ginger: 1 tablespoon (minced)
- Garlic cloves: three (minced)
- Small head cauliflower: one (bite-size florets)
- Chili powder: two teaspoons
- Ground coriander: one teaspoon
- Red curry paste: three tablespoons
- Can coconut milk: one (14-ounce)
- Lime: one (halved)
- Can chickpeas: one (28-ounces)
- Frozen peas: one and a half cups
- Freshly ground black pepper and kosher salt
- Steamed rice: (optional) for serving
- Fresh cilantro: ¼ cup (chopped)
- Scallions: four (thinly sliced)

Instructions:

1. Over medium flame in a large saucepan, heat the olive oil. Cook until onion and bell pepper are nearly tender.

Add the ginger and garlic and cook for one minute.

2. Add in the cauliflower and toss well. Cook, until the chili powder, coriander, and red curry paste begin to caramelize.

3. Add the coconut milk and bring the mixture to a boil. Cover the saucepan and cook until the cauliflower is tender.

4. Season with salt and pepper, and add the chickpeas and peas.

5. If needed, serve with rice. Garnish with cilantro and scallions.

2.2: Thai Peanut Coconut Cauliflower Chickpea Curry

Preparation time: 15 minutes

Cooking time: 15 minutes

Servings: 4

Ingredients

- For the curry:
- Coconut oil: half tablespoon
- Garlic cloves: three (minced)
- Fresh ginger: one tablespoon (grated)
- Large carrot: one (thinly sliced)
- Cauliflower: one small head (three-four cups)
- Green onions: one bunch (diced)
- Coconut milk: one can (lite) (15 ounces)
- Vegetarian broth or water: one-third cup
- Red curry paste: 2 tablespoons
- Natural creamy peanut butter (or cashew butter): 2 tablespoons
- Gluten-free soy sauce or coconut aminos: half tablespoon
- Mccormick Ground turmeric: half teaspoon
- Mccormick ground red cayenne pepper: half teaspoon (plus more if you like extra heat)
- Salt: half teaspoon
- Red pepper: one (julienned)
- Chickpeas: one can (15 ounces) (rinsed and drained)
- Frozen peas: half cup
- To garnish:

- Fresh cilantro
- Green onion
- Peanuts or cashews (chopped)

Instructions

1. Heat a large pot. Cook coconut oil, garlic, and ginger for 30 seconds before adding the green onion, carrot, and cauliflower florets.
2. Then, whisk together the coconut milk, soy sauce/coconut aminos, water, turmeric, peanut butter, red cayenne pepper, curry paste, and salt.
3. Then add the bell pepper and chickpeas and cook for 10 minutes.
4. Stir in the frozen peas and cook for another minute.
5. Add chopped peanuts/cashews, green onion, and cilantro to garnish.

2.3: Stir-Fried Courgettes and Egg Recipe

Preparation time: 10 minutes

Cooking time: 5 minutes

Serving: 1

Ingredients

- Courgette: one (peeled and diced)
- Eggs: two
- Water: two tablespoons
- Soy sauce: one tablespoon
- Oyster sauce: half tablespoon
- Finely chopped garlic: two cloves
- Sugar: half tablespoon

Instructions

1. In a wok, heat two tablespoons of cooking oil over high heat.
2. Add chopped garlic cloves and fry for about 15 seconds.

3. Add one peeled and diced courgette and stir fry for one minute with the garlic.

4. 2: Move the courgettes to one side of the wok and crack two eggs into the clear side. Scrambled the eggs for a few seconds before being combined with the courgettes.

5. 3: In a wok, combine half tablespoon sugar, one tablespoon soy sauce, half tablespoon oyster sauce, and two tablespoon water. Stir fry for another 2 to 3 minutes, or until the courgettes have softened and absorbed the sauce's flavor. Then serve with a side of steamed rice.

2.4: Bangkok Coconut Curry Noodle Bowls

Preparation time: 20 minutes

Cooking time: 40 minutes

Servings: 4

Ingredients

- For the coconut curry sauce:
- Oil: one tablespoon
- Shallots: two
- Fresh ginger: one tablespoon minced (or a paste)
- Red curry paste: two tablespoons
- Regular coconut milk: one can (14-ounce)
- Reduced sodium chicken or veggie broth: half cup (optional)
- Sugar: three tablespoons
- Hot chili paste: one tablespoon
- Fish sauce: two tablespoons
- Soy sauce: two tablespoons
- For the bowls:
- Rice noodles: 4-ounces (brown rice noodles)
- Oil: one tablespoon
- Onion: half (chopped)
- Broccoli florets: one cup (chopped)
- Carrots: one cup (shredded)
- Asparagus: one cup (chopped)
- Purple cabbage: one cup (shredded)
- Sesame seeds: for topping

- Limes: for serving
- Fresh basil: handful for serving

Instructions

Noodles:

1. In cold water, soak the noodles for a few minutes.

2. Start right away; they will need to soak for at least 20 minutes.

3. Drain and rinse when they are soft.

Sauce:

1. In a big saucepan, heat the oil.

2. Stir in the shallots and ginger for 3-5 minutes.

3. Stir in the curry paste for one minute.

4. Combine the sugar, coconut milk, chili paste, soy sauce, and fish sauce in a large mixing bowl.

5. Simmer for about 15 minutes.

Assembly and Vegetables:

1. Heat the oil in a big skillet over a high flame.

2. Combine the asparagus, carrots, onion, and broccoli in a large mixing bowl.

3. Stir fry the broccoli and asparagus for about 5 minutes, or until they are beautiful bright green.

4. Then, put the noodles in the pan with the vegetables and toss to combine.

5. Serve with purple cabbage and sesame seeds on top, as well as a squeeze of lime or basil leaves if desired.

2.5: Healing Lemongrass Chickpea Thai Green Curry

Preparation time: 15 minutes

Cooking time: 45 minutes

Servings: 4

Ingredients

- For the brown rice:
- Coconut oil: one teaspoon
- Uncooked short grain brown rice: one cup
- For the Thai green curry:
- Olive oil or coconut oil: two teaspoons
- Garlic cloves: three (minced)
- Green onion: ¾ cup (diced)
- Lemongrass: two stalks (tender white inner bulb only and minced)
- Carrots: one cup (diced)
- Ginger: one tablespoon (freshly minced)
- Fresh basil: three tablespoons (finely diced)
- Green curry paste: 2 tablespoons
- Turmeric: half teaspoon
- Lite coconut milk: one can (15-ounce)
- Vegetarian broth or water: half cup
- Chickpeas: one can (15 ounces) (rinsed and drained)
- Gluten-free soy sauce or coconut aminos: one tablespoon
- Lime: one (juiced)
- Salt: half teaspoon (plus more to taste)
- Red bell pepper: one (thinly sliced)
- Frozen peas: one cup
- Cilantro, green onion & hot sauce: to garnish

Instructions

1. Over medium heat, toast the rice for 5 minutes or until fragrant.

2. Add 2 ½ cups water to a pot and bring to a boil.

3. Reduce heat to medium, cover, and cook for 45 minutes.

4. Heat the oil over medium-high heat in a large pot. Add garlic, diced fresh basil, green onion, fresh ginger lemongrass, and carrots to the hot oil. Stir fry for five minutes.

5. Add in the green curry paste and turmeric for 30 seconds to release the flavors.

6. Combine the coconut milk, vegetarian broth, lime juice, chickpeas, salt, red bell pepper, and soy sauce in a large mixing bowl.

7. Cover and cook for 20 minutes.

8. Stir in frozen peas just before serving.

9. Toss over brown rice in a bowl and top with fresh cilantro, green onion, and a splash of hot sauce, if desired.

2.6: Creamy Thai Sweet Potato Curry

Preparation time: 10 minutes

Cooking time: 20 minutes

Servings: 4-5

Ingredients

- Oil: one tablespoon
- Shallots: two (thinly sliced)
- Sweet potatoes: two (peeled and cubed)
- Fresh baby spinach: 3-4 cups
- Curry paste: 2-3 tablespoons
- Regular coconut milk: one (14 ounces)
- Broth or water: half- one cup
- Peanuts and cilantro: half cup (chopped)
- Soy sauce: to taste

Instructions

1. Garlic, shallots, and ginger should all be roasted. In a food processor, mix all of the ingredients and some spices, lemongrass paste, and cilantro.

2. Heat the oil to a medium-high temperature.

3. Stir in the shallots and sweet potatoes to coat them in oil.

4. Stir in the curry paste until it is well mixed.

5. Add the spinach until it is fully wilted.

6. Half of the peanut/cilantro mixture should be added; the remainder should be saved for topping.

7. Add soy sauce.

8. Serve with the remaining peanuts/cilantro on top of the rice.

2.7: Red Curry with Vegetables

Preparation time: 10 minutes

Cooking time: 30 minutes

Servings: 4

Ingredients

- Brown jasmine rice or long-grain brown rice: one ¼ cups (rinsed)
- Coconut oil or olive oil: one tablespoon
- Small white onion: one cup (chopped)
- Salt: a pinch (more to taste)
- Finely grated fresh ginger: 1 tablespoon
- Garlic cloves: two (pressed or minced)
- Red bell pepper: one (sliced into thin 2-inch long strips)
- Yellow, orange, or green bell pepper: one (sliced into thin 2-inch long strips)
- Carrots: three (one cup) (peeled and sliced)
- Thai red curry paste: two tablespoons
- Regular coconut milk: one can (14 ounces)
- Water: half cup
- Packed thinly sliced kale: one and a half cups (tough ribs removed first)
- Coconut sugar or brown sugar: one and a half teaspoons
- Tamari or soy sauce: one tablespoon
- Rice vinegar or fresh lime juice: two teaspoons

- Garnishes/sides: fresh basil/cilantro/red pepper flakes (chopped) sriracha/chili garlic sauce (optional)

Instructions

1. Boil rice in a big pot of water. Rinse and season the rice with salt and fluff it with a fork just before serving.

2. Preheat a broad skillet.

3. Add the oil, a pinch of salt, and the onion and cook, frequently stirring, for about 5 minutes.

4. Add ginger and garlic and cook for about 30 seconds.

5. Toss in the carrots and bell peppers. Cook for another 3 to 5 minutes.

6. After that, add the curry paste and cook for two minutes, stirring frequently.

7. Combine the coconut milk, water, kale, and sugar in a mixing bowl. Let the mixture simmer over medium flame.

8. Season with tamari and rice vinegar. To taste, season with salt.

9. To serve, divide the rice and curry among bowls and top with chopped cilantro and a pinch of red pepper flakes, if desired.

10. Serve with sriracha or chili garlic sauce on the side if you like curries spicy.

2.8: Thai Red Curry with Asparagus and Tofu

Preparation time: 30 minutes

Cooking time: 20 minutes

Servings: 4

Ingredients
- Peanut oil canola or vegetable oil: one tablespoon
- Extra-firm tofu pressed for 30 minutes: 14 oz (cut into triangles)
- light unsweetened coconut milk: one can (13.5 ounces)

- Red curry paste: ¼ cup
- Vegetable broth: ¾ cup
- Soy sauce or tamari: 2 teaspoons
- Light brown sugar: one tablespoon
- Red bell pepper: one (thinly sliced)
- Asparagus: one lb (tough ends removed and cut into 1-inch pieces)
- Cooked rice or rice noodles
- Cilantro leaves
- Lime wedges

Instructions

1. In a pan, heat the peanut oil over medium-high heat. Cook for five minutes with tofu triangles and then flip and cook for another five minutes on the other side. Set aside.

2. Add half a cup of coconut milk and cook until the coconut milk has thickened.

3. Stir in the red curry paste and cook for one minute.

4. Combine the remaining coconut milk, broth, soy sauce, and sugar in a mixing bowl. When the sauce has reached a boil, add the red pepper and the asparagus and cook for three minutes.

5. Return the tofu to the skillet and stir until it is fully covered in curry sauce.

6. Remove from flame and serve with cilantro and lime wedges on top of noodles or rice.

2.9: Green Curry Noodle Soup

Preparation time: 10 minutes

Cooking time: 15 minutes

Servings: 3

Ingredients

- Olive oil: one tablespoon
- Extra fat shallot: one-two (finely diced)
- Green curry paste: ¼ - ½ cup (make your own)
- Chicken or veggie broth: 4 cups
- Optional additions (jarred curry paste) – four-inch stock of lemongrass, smashed, three-four slices galangal, four-six kefir lime leaves)
- Crispy tofu: eight ounces
- Broccolini: eight ounces (cut in half lengthwise)
- Coconut milk: one can (13.5 ounces)
- Fish sauce/vegan fish sauce: two-four teaspoons
- Half lime: juice (more to taste)
- Basil leaves: ¼ - ½ cup (packed)
- Dry rice noodles: six-eight ounces (cooked according to directions on package)
- Bean sprouts/lime wedges/scallions and fresh basil: for garnishing

Instructions:

1. In a medium wok, heat the oil and cook the shallot until golden.

2. Sauté for 1-2 minutes with the curry paste.

3. Add a 4 inch stock of smashed lemongrass, three slices galangal, and 3-4 kefir lime leaves while using a jarred green curry paste.

4. Simmer until the broccolini is only tender and bright green. Add the coconut milk and tofu at this point if using.

5. Combine the fish sauce and lime juice in a mixing bowl.

6. To brighten the soup, combine 1 cup of coconut broth with the fresh basil in a blender and puree until smooth and bright green.

7. Adjust the lime, salt, and spice to taste.

8. Using 3-4 bowls, divide the noodles. Pour the flavorful broth on top of it. Bean sprouts, lime wedges, scallions, and chili flakes may be added as a garnish.

2.10: Easy Thai Curry Hot Pot

Preparation time: 25 minutes

Cooking time: 10 minutes

Servings: 8-10

Ingredients

- Hot pot broth ingredients:
- Olive oil: one tablespoon
- Garlic cloves: five (minced)
- Fresh ginger: one inch (cut into thick slices)
- Kitchen basics vegetable stock: eight cups
- Coconut milk: three cans (15 ounces)
- Thai Kitchen red curry paste: four-six tablespoons (to taste)
- Hot pot dippers and topping ingredients (pick your faves!)
- Protein
- Crispy tofu
- Noodles / rice
- Cooked rice noodles (any width), brown or white rice, quinoa/any other favorite grains/chickpeas in place of noodles
- Veggies
- Sliced bell peppers, sweet potatoes, broccoli, carrots, onions (red, white, or yellow), peas, cauliflower, squash, mushrooms
- Greens
- Cabbage, baby bok choy, kale, spinach, or collards
- Toppings
- Fresh herbs (Thai basil (chopped), chives/cilantro)

- Fresh chiles (serrano peppers/dried crushed red peppers, Thai bird chiles)
- Toasted coconut flakes
- Lime wedges
- Green onions: thinly sliced

Instructions:

1. To make the hot pot broth:

2. In a huge stockpot, heat the olive oil.

3. Add the garlic and ginger and cook.

4. Stir in the vegetable stock and coconut milk until all is well combined.

5. Then whisk in 3 to 4 tablespoons of curry paste until it has completely dissolved.

6. Taste, and if necessary, add more curry paste.

7. Cover and cook for 5 minutes on low heat. After that, take out the ginger slices.

8. Simmer until ready to serve.

9. Add your preferred dippers, boil and strain them into the bowls using a strainer. Fill each serving bowl with a ladleful of broth.

10. Garnish with preferred toppings and serve hot.

2.11: Thai Yellow Curry with Chickpeas and Cauliflower

Preparation time: 5 minutes

Cooking time: 25 minutes

Servings: 4

Ingredients:
- Curry
- Water (or coconut oil): two tablespoons
- Shallot: 1/3 cup (chopped)
- Garlic: four cloves (minced)
- Fresh ginger: two tablespoons (minced)
- Small serrano pepper: one (seeds removed, finely chopped)
- Red or yellow curry paste: three-four tablespoons
- Light coconut milk: two cups
- Ground turmeric: one teaspoon
- Maple syrup: one tablespoon (plus more to taste)
- Coconut aminos: two tablespoons (or sub tamari or soy sauce, plus more to taste)
- Cauliflower: one cup (chopped)
- Cooked chickpeas: 1 ¼ cup (rinsed and drained)
- Salad / bowl optional
- Cauliflower rice, quinoa, or rice
- Avocado
- Greens
- Lime wedges
- Cilantro
- Sesame seeds

Instructions

1. In a large pan over medium heat, add the shallot, garlic, ginger, and serrano pepper, along with a splash of water or coconut oil.

2. Cook, constantly stirring, for 2-3 minutes.

3. Stir in the curry paste.

4. Stir in coconut milk, turmeric, maple syrup, or coconut sugar (if desired), and coconut aminos (or tamari). Over medium heat, bring to a simmer.

5. After the cauliflower and chickpeas have begun to soften, reduce the heat slightly.

6. To make the chickpeas and cauliflower soft and fill them with curry taste, cover and cook for 10-15 minutes, stirring occasionally. Keep it at a low simmer; if it starts to boil, turn down the flame.

7. At this stage, taste the broth and make any necessary adjustments to the flavor.

8. Serve over rice, quinoa, or greens as is (optional).

9. Toppings such as lime, cilantro, diced red onion, or sesame seeds may be added as needed (optional).

2.12: Real Veggie Pad Thai (Vegan/Gluten-Free)

Preparation time: 20 minutes

Cooking time: 10 minutes

Servings: 4

Ingredients

- For the pad thai:
- Wide rice noodles: 200 grams (7 oz)
- Peanut oil: two tablespoons
- Spring onions: two (sliced)
- Garlic cloves: one-two (finely sliced)
- Hot red chili: one (finely sliced)
- Small broccoli: half (cut into florets)
- Red pepper: one (finely sliced)
- Carrots: two (shaved into ribbons with a speed peeler)
- Roasted & unsalted peanuts: ¼ cup (30 grams, crushed)
- Fresh cilantro: one handful (to garnish)
- Lime: one to serve (optional)
- For the sauce:
- Gluten-free soy sauce: five tablespoons
- Maple syrup: two-three tablespoons (adjust to taste)

Instructions:

1. Cook rice noodles, drain, then toss with a little oil to keep them from sticking together and set aside.

2. In a frying pan, heat one tablespoon of oil.

3. Add the spring onions, garlic, and chili, and continue to stir until fragrant.

4. Place in a separate serving bowl.

5. In the same wok/frying pan, heat another tablespoon of oil and stir-fry broccoli for about 2 minutes.

6. Stir in the red pepper and carrot ribbons until they are cooked but still crunchy.

7. Place all of the vegetables in a separate bowl.

8. In a small cup, combine all of the sauce ingredients and pour the sauce into the wok/frying pan's bottom.

9. Add the noodles and toss them in with the sauce. Stir in the spring onions, chilies, garlic, and stir-fried vegetables, and let it warm up for a minute or two.

10. Serve in plates with crushed peanuts, fresh cilantro, and lime juice, if desired.

2.13: Thai Green Vegetable Curry

Preparation time: 15 minutes

Cooking time: 40 minutes

Servings: 4

Ingredients

- Vegetable oil: two tablespoons
- Shallots: three (finely sliced)
- Thai green curry paste: four tablespoons
- Red chili: one (deseeded and finely chopped)
- Butternut squash: 350 grams (peeled and cut into cubes)
- Large red pepper: one (deseeded and cut into thick slices)
- Full fat coconut milk: 400gram can
- Dried kaffir lime leaves: five
- Mangetout: 150gram
- Baby corn: 100gram (halved lengthways)
- Small bunch coriander: one (roughly chopped)
- Cooked rice and lime wedges: to serve

Instructions:

1. In a big pan, heat the oil.

2. Cook for 7-10 minutes with the shallots and a pinch of salt.

3. Cook for 2 minutes after adding the curry paste and chili to the bowl.

4. Add the squash, pepper, and coconut milk, along with 200ml water, and mix to combine. Cook for almost 15-20 mins after adding the lime leaves.

5. Stir the mangetout and baby corn into the curry, then cover and cook until the vegetables are just tender.

6. Season with salt and pepper, then mix in half of the coriander. Remove and discard the lime leaves.

2.14: Thai Chilli Broccoli Salad Recipe

Preparation time: 15 minutes

Cooking time: 15 minutes

Servings: 4

Ingredients:
- Blanched broccoli florets: half kg
- For the chili vinaigrette:
- Lemon juice: one tablespoon
- Pomegranate juice: one tablespoon
- Castor sugar: half teaspoon
- Crushed yellow mustard seeds: one teaspoon
- Dried chili flakes: ¼ teaspoon
- Chopped garlic: one teaspoon
- Oil: one tablespoon
- Segmented orange: one
- For the curd topping:
- Hung curd: two tablespoons
- Grated rind of orange: one
- Orange juice: two tablespoons
- Vinegar: one tablespoon
- Tomato puree: one teaspoon
- Sugar, salt, and pepper: one teaspoon

Instructions:

1. Combine all vinaigrette ingredients in a mixing bowl.

2. Set aside for 2–3 hours.

3. Combine the curd topping with the ingredients and season to taste.

4. Toss the broccoli with the vinaigrette and top with the curd dressing and orange section just before serving.

2.15: Thai Pomelo Salad Recipe

Preparation time: 5 minutes

Cooking time: 5 minutes

Servings: 2

Ingredients:

- Red chili (dried and fresh)
- Onion: four tablespoons (minced)
- Garlic: one tablespoon (minced)
- Shallots: two tablespoons
- Sugar: half teaspoon
- Shredded coconut: ¾ cup
- Vegan fish sauce: to taste
- Lime juice: to taste
- Peanuts: half cup
- Tamarind concentrate or pulp: one tablespoon
- Pomelo: 1.5 lb
- Coconut oil: half teaspoon
- Coriander: a fresh handful

Instructions:

1. Dry-roast the dried red chili, then mix it with some onion and garlic to make a paste.

2. Put the paste, sugar, lime juice, tamarind, and vegan fish sauce in a saucepan and cook until the sugar has dissolved.

3. Adjust the flavors

4. Allow the dressing to cool as you prepare the salad.

5. Dry-roast the shredded coconut for a few minutes before proceeding to the peanuts.

6. In a little amount of oil, fry the shallots and garlic until crispy, then drain on kitchen paper.

7. Prepare your pomelo by removing the flesh and placing it in a big mixing bowl. Add some new red chili powder, roasted peanuts, some garlic and shallots, and just enough dressing to cover anything. Get your hands dirty and gently combine everything! Serve straight away, topped with some torn coriander leaf and the remaining shallots and garlic.

2.16: Roasted Thai Yellow Curry Potatoes

Preparation time: 10 minutes

Cooking time: 40 minutes

Marinate time: 30 minutes

Servings: 4

Ingredients

- Yukon Gold potatoes: two lbs
- Coconut oil: three tablespoons
- Thai yellow curry paste: two tablespoons
- Salt: one teaspoon
- Freshly ground black pepper: to taste
- Cilantro leaves: one tablespoon (for garnish)

Instructions

1. Preheat oven to 400 degrees Fahrenheit.

2. In a large bowl, place the diced potatoes.

3. Combine the coconut oil, salt, and yellow curry paste in a small bowl. Mix thoroughly.

4. Over the potatoes, pour the curry paste mixture.

5. Allow 30 minutes for the potatoes to marinate.

6. Spread the potatoes in a single layer on parchment paper on a baking tray, then season with ground black pepper.

7. Remove the pan from the oven after 20 minutes to stir.

8. Place the potatoes into the oven again for a final 20 minutes of baking.

9. Just before eating, garnish with cilantro leaves. Have fun!

2.17: Smashed Potatoes with Thai-Style Chile and Herb Sauce

Preparation time: 20 minutes

Cooking time: 60 minutes

Servings: 4-6

Ingredients

- Olive oil: four tablespoons
- Small new or Yukon gold potatoes: two pounds
- Kosher salt
- Fish sauce: two tablespoons
- Lime juice: two tablespoons
- Rice vinegar: two tablespoons
- Minced Fresno or serrano chile: one tablespoon or red-pepper flakes: half teaspoon (plus more to taste)
- Soy sauce or tamari: one teaspoon
- Granulated sugar: one teaspoon
- Garlic clove: one (grated)
- Roughly chopped fresh cilantro: ¼ cup (plus whole leaves for serving)
- Thinly sliced scallions: ¼ cup (white and green parts)

Instructions:

1. Preheat the oven to 450 degrees Fahrenheit.

2. Brush the sheet pan all over with one tablespoon olive oil.

3. Boil the potatoes with 1 inch and two tablespoons salt in a huge pot.

4. Continue to cook, uncovered, 15 to 18 minutes, or until the potatoes are fork-tender. Drain the cooked potatoes in a colander.

5. Meanwhile, combine the fish sauce, soy sauce, lime juice, chile, rice vinegar, sugar, and garlic in a small cup, then add the scallions and cilantro.

6. Put the potatoes on the prepared sheet pan.

7. Gently smash each potato with the bottom of a measuring cup until it is around 1/2-inch thick. Drizzle the remaining three tablespoons of olive oil over the potatoes and flip to coat both sides evenly.

8. Roast for 30 to 40 minutes, until golden brown and crisp, after seasoning with 1/2 teaspoon salt.

9. Place the potatoes on a serving platter, season lightly with salt, and pour the sauce over them. Serve immediately, garnished with cilantro leaves.

Chapter 3: Quick and Easy Dinner Recipes

Thai recipes are known for their freshness, exotic scents, and lavish spices. Here, I will show you some simple vegetarian Thai dishes that you can make at home for dinner.

3.1: Spaghetti Squash Pad Thai

Preparation time: 10 minutes

Cooking time: 40 minutes

Servings: 4-6

Ingredients

- For the sauce:
- Tamari/soy sauce: three tablespoons
- Sweet chili sauce: three tablespoons
- Rice wine vinegar: one tablespoon
- For the pad Thai:
- Spaghetti squash: one medium
- Extra-virgin olive oil: (for drizzling)
- Sea salt: (for seasoning)
- Roasted peanut oil: two tablespoons
- Extra-firm tofu: 14-ounces (drained, pressed, and cubed)
- Cornstarch: two tablespoons
- Broccoli: one small head (only florets and chopped)
- Scallions: five (sliced)
- Garlic cloves: three medium (minced)
- Bean sprouts: one heaping cup
- For serving:
- Sriracha
- Roasted peanuts: (crushed)
- Lime wedges
- Fresh cilantro: (chopped)

Instructions:

1. Preheat the oven to 400 degrees Fahrenheit.

2. Scrape the seeds out of the spaghetti squash by slicing it in half lengthwise. Drizzle with olive oil, season with salt, and put cut side up on the baking sheet. Roast for one hour, or until fork-tender. Pour off any remaining

liquid, then scrape the spaghetti squash into strands with a fork. Set it aside.

3. **Create the sauce in the meantime:** In a small mixing bowl, combine all of the ingredients and stir to combine. Set aside.
4. Over medium heat, heat a large skillet. Toss the tofu in the cornstarch in a mixing bowl. Cook the tofu in the skillet with the peanut oil until golden.
5. Add the broccoli and cook for three minutes.
6. Combine the bean sprouts, scallions, spaghetti squash, and garlic in a large mixing bowl.
7. Stir in the sauce to cover the noodles uniformly.
8. Serve with lime wedges, peanuts, sriracha, and cilantro on the side.

3.2: Steamed Dumplings with Shiitake Mushrooms, Ginger, and Coriander

Preparation time: 25 minutes

Cooking time: 20 minutes

Servings: 4

Ingredients

- Dumpling wrappers: one package (round and frozen)
- Banana leaf: one (for steaming) (easily available frozen at most food stores)
- For the filling:
- Shitake mushrooms: three cups (fresh and sliced)
- Tofu: one cup (cubed, medium-firm)
- Galangal: one-two inch piece (or sliced ginger)
- Garlic: three-four cloves
- Spring onions: two (sliced)
- Cilantro: half cup (leaves and stems) (fresh and chopped)
- White pepper: ¼ teaspoon
- Soy sauce: three tablespoons
- Sesame oil: two tablespoons
- Chili sauce: one teaspoon (or more if you want them spicy)
- Vegetarian chicken stock/vegetable stock: ¼ cup
- For the dumplings:
- Cornstarch/flour: one-two tablespoon
- Soy sauce: for garnishing

Instructions:

1. Allow at least 30 minutes for the banana leaf to thaw.
2. Line a steamer with one or two layers of banana leaves (keep dumplings from sticking).
3. In a food processor, combine all filling ingredients and process until very finely chopped but not a paste.
4. Place six dumpling wrappers on a clean work surface at once. Prepare a small bowl of water for sealing the dumplings as well.

5. One teaspoon of the filling should be placed in the center of each wrapper. Then moisten the outside of the wrapper with your fingers (or a pastry brush) dipped in water.
6. To close the wrapper, bring the sides up over the filling and press together. To make a decorative edge, pinch along the seam.
7. Immediately steam the dumplings, or cover and chill for up to 3 hours.
8. Steam the dumplings, put them in a banana leaf-lined steamer (they can touch), and steam for 15 to 20 minutes until the mushrooms are cooked through.
9. Toss with soy sauce and chili sauce before serving.

3.3: Thai Pumpkin Curry (Vegan/Gluten-Free)

Preparation time: 20 minutes

Cooking time: 10 minutes

Servings: 4

Ingredients

- For the Pumpkin:
- Pumpkin: half small (or acorn squash, orange squash, or butternut)
- Yam: one small (or one sweet potato) (peeled and cubed)
- Medium carrots: one-two (thick slices)
- Yellow bell pepper: one (bite-sized pieces)
- Cherry tomatoes: one cup
- Chickpeas: half can (drained)
- Orange zest: two tablespoons
- For the Curry Sauce:
- Garlic: three-four cloves
- Red chilies: one-two
- Coconut milk: one can
- Tamarind paste: one teaspoon
- Soy sauce: two and a half tablespoons
- Brown sugar: one tablespoon
- Lime juice: one tablespoon
- Orange juice: two tablespoons (fresh)
- Turmeric: half teaspoon
- Rice vinegar: one tablespoon
- Coriander seeds: one tablespoon (ground)
- Cumin: one tablespoon
- Fennel seed: one teaspoon
- Purple onion: 1/3 (sliced)
- Basil leaves: for garnish (a handful fresh)
- Roasted pumpkin seeds: one tablespoon (for garnish)

Instructions:

1. In a food processor, combine all sauce ingredients. Process all thoroughly.

2. Cut the pumpkin or squash open and scoop out the seeds with a spoon to prepare it. Remove the skin from the pumpkin and cut it into cubes.
3. Prepare the remaining vegetables, as well as the rind from the orange.
4. Over medium-high heat, combine the carrots, pumpkin, and yam with the curry sauce in a wok or frying pan.
5. Reduce heat to medium when the curry starts to simmer, let the vegetables get soft.
6. Stir in the bell pepper, orange rind, chickpeas, and cherry tomatoes. Cook for another 2 minutes.
7. Check for salt and spice with a tasting.
8. Fresh basil leaves and pumpkin seeds can be sprinkled on top. Serve with Thai jasmine rice.

3.4: Authentic Thai Tofu Satay (Vegetarian/Vegan)

Preparation time: 20 minutes

Cooking time: 15 minutes

Servings: 2-4

Ingredients
- Satay
- Firm Tofu: 14 oz (frozen and thawed)
- Full-fat Coconut Milk: ¼ cup
- Garlic cloves: three (minced)
- Ginger: two teaspoons (grated)
- Curry Paste: one tablespoon
- Maple Syrup: one tablespoon
- Low-sodium Soy Sauce: two tablespoon
- Bamboo Skewers: ten
- Cilantro: to taste
- Lime: to taste
- Peanuts: for garnish (chopped)
- Peanut Sauce
- Creamy Peanut Butter: ¼ cup
- Warm Water: two tablespoons

- Curry Paste: one tablespoon
- Maple Syrup: one tablespoon
- Soy Sauce: half tablespoon
- Rice Vinegar: half tablespoon
- Lime Juice: one tablespoon
- Garlic: half teaspoon (minced)
- Sesame Oil: half teaspoon
- Sriracha: half tablespoon

Instructions

1. In a mixing bowl, combine the marinade ingredients, then add the thawed tofu and gently stir to cover all bits.
2. Preheat the oven to 400 degrees Fahrenheit. Tear the marinated tofu into small pieces and thread them onto skewers.
3. Bake for 30-35 minutes on a parchment-lined baking sheet, flipping halfway through.
4. Switch on the broiler for 4-5 minutes, in the end, to enable the skewers to crisp and grow charred edges (do not burn!).
5. In a small cup, whisk together all of the ingredients for the peanut sauce until smooth.
6. Serve satay drizzled with sauce and garnished with minced cilantro and peanuts.

3.5: Thai Stir-Fried Noodles with Vegetables

Preparation time: 15 minutes

Cooking time: 12 minutes

Servings: 3-4

Ingredients

- Chinese-style wheat noodles: five-eight ounces (or egg noodles)
- Vegetable oil: two-three tablespoons (for stir-frying)
- Garlic cloves: four (minced)
- Galangal/ginger: two-three tablespoon (grated)
- Shallots/purple onion: ¼ cup (chopped)
- Carrot: one (sliced)
- Shiitake mushrooms: five-eight (sliced)
- Broccoli: one small head (chopped into florets)
- Red pepper: one small (sliced)
- Bean sprouts: two cups
- Garnish: fresh coriander/basil
- Stir-fry Sauce:
- Fresh lime juice: three tablespoons (or more to taste)
- Soy sauce: three tablespoons (or more to taste)
- Fish sauce: one tablespoon (or more to taste)
- Rice vinegar: three tablespoons (or white wine vinegar)
- Oyster sauce: three tablespoons
- Teaspoons sugar: one and a half-two teaspoons (or more to taste)
- White pepper: ¼ tablespoon
- Dried crushed chili: ½ - ¾ teaspoon (or more to taste)

Instructions:

1. Cook the noodles until they are al dente in lightly salted water, drain and rinse with cold water.
2. In a cup, combine all of the ingredients for the stir-fry sauce, stirring well to melt the sugar. Set aside.

3. Over medium-high heat, heat a wok or a big frying pan.
4. Stir-fry the garlic, shallot, and ginger for 1 minute in the oil.
5. Add the carrots and 1 to 2 tablespoons of the stir-fry sauce you made earlier.
6. Stir-fry until carrots are slightly softened.
7. Add 3 to 4 teaspoons of the stir-fry sauce plus the red pepper, broccoli, and mushrooms.
8. Continue to stir-fry until the mushrooms and red pepper soften and the broccoli turns bright green but still crisp.
9. Combine the noodles and the remaining stir-fry sauce in a large mixing bowl.
10. Fold in the bean sprouts during the last minute of cooking.
11. Adjust the flavors.
12. Serve immediately in bowls or plates with fresh coriander or basil sprinkled on top.

3.6: Easy Thai Rice Noodles with Basil

Preparation time: 12 minutes

Cooking time: 5 minutes

Servings: 2-4

Ingredients
- Thai rice noodles: six-ten ounces
- Vegetable oil: two tablespoons (for stir-frying)
- For the Toppings:
- One handful basil: for garnishing (fresh)
- One handful of Cashews: for garnishing (chopped/ground)
- For the Basil Sauce:
- Basil: half cup (fresh)
- Dry cashews: 1/3 cup (dry roasted and unsalted)
- Garlic cloves: three-four

- Coconut/olive oil: four tablespoons
- Lime juice: one tablespoon (freshly squeezed)
- Fish sauce/soy sauce for vegetarians: one tablespoon
- One chili: optional

Instructions:

1. Bring the water to a boil in a pot, remove it from the heat, and add the noodles.
2. When you are making the sauce, soak the noodles.
3. The noodles should then be drained and rinsed with cold water to avoid sticking.
4. In a mini-chopper, combine all basil sauce ingredients and blitz all together.
5. Over medium-high heat, pour in the oil in a big frying pan and whisk it around before adding the noodles.
6. Add two tablespoons of the sauce or until desired softness is achieved.
7. Remove the pan from the heat. Toss in the remaining sauce to evenly disperse it.
8. Taste it and adjust the flavors.
9. Serve with a sprinkling of fresh basil and chopped or ground cashews.

3.7: Thai Heavenly Pineapple Fried Rice

Preparation time: 30 minutes

Cooking time: 10 minutes

Servings: 5

Ingredients

- Pineapple chunks: one small can (drained)/ fresh pineapple chunks: one and a half cup
- Cooked rice: three-four cups (would prefer several days old)
- Vegetable/faux chicken stock: ¼ cup
- Shallots: two (finely chopped)
- Garlic cloves: three (finely chopped)
- Red or green chili: one (thinly sliced)
- Frozen peas: half cup
- Carrot: one small (grated)
- Currants/raisins: ¼ cup
- Unsalted Whole cashews: ½ cup (roasted)
- Onions: three (finely sliced)
- Coriander: 1/3 cup (fresh)
- Stir-fry sauce:
- Soy sauce: three tablespoons
- Curry powder: two teaspoons
- Sugar: half teaspoon (optional)

Instructions:

1. Toss one tablespoon oil with the rice, breaking up any lumps with your fingertips, and set aside.
2. Combine the soy sauce and curry powder in a cup and whisk to combine.
3. In a wok/large frying pan over medium-high heat, drizzle 1-2 tablespoons of oil.
4. Stir in the chili, garlic, and shallots until fragrant, around 1 minute.
5. Stir in the peas and carrots.

6. Combine the pineapple chunks, rice, currants, peas, and cashews in a mixing bowl.
7. Drizzle the fish/soy sauce mixture with the curry powder over the top and stir-fry to combine for 5 to 8 minutes.
8. Switch off the burner. Taste and adjust the flavors.
9. Suppose serving at a party, into a carved-out pineapple). Serve with coriander and spring onions, and ENJOY!

3.8: Easy Thai Coconut Rice

Preparation time: 5 minutes

Cooking time: 20 minutes

Servings: 4

Ingredients
- Coconut oil/vegetable oil: half teaspoon
- Thai jasmine white rice: two cups (rinsed well)
- Coconut milk: two cups (canned)
- Salt: half teaspoon
- Cups water: one ¾ cups

Instructions:

1. In a deep-sided pot, rub the oil all over the rim.
2. In a large pot, combine the rice, salt, coconut milk, and water.
3. Stop stirring until the liquid has started to bubble gently.
4. Cover tightly with a lid and cook until the rice has absorbed most of the liquid.
5. Pull the rice aside with a fork to see if it is cooked.
6. Steam for a few minutes longer if there is still a lot of liquid lefts. Turn off the heat when the liquid is gone.
7. Keep the covered pot on the hot burner for another 5 to 10 minutes, or until you are ready to eat, with the heat turned off.

8. Taste for salt, and if necessary, add a pinch more. Combine the rice with your favorite dishes for a delicious meal.

3.9: Thai Yellow Rice

Preparation time: 10 minutes

Cooking time: 20 minutes

Servings: 4-5

Ingredients

- Vegetable oil: two tablespoons
- Onion: ¼ cup (finely chopped)
- Garlic cloves: three (minced)
- Chili flakes: 1/8-1/4 teaspoons (or cayenne pepper)
- Red pepper: ¼ cup (diced)
- Roma tomato: one (diced)
- White Thai jasmine rice: two cups (white basmati rice, uncooked)
- Chicken stock: 4 cups
- Lime: one (juiced)
- Fish sauce: two tablespoons (or soy sauce)
- Turmeric: half teaspoons
- Saffron: 1/3-1/4 teaspoon (optional)
- Frozen peas: ¼ cup
- Salt: to taste
- Fresh basil: a handful (for garnish)

Instructions:

1. Preheat a large pot over high heat.

2. Pour in the oil and give it a good swirl.

3. After that, toss in the chili, onion, and garlic.

4. After that, add the tomato and red pepper.

5. Stir in the rice to evenly coat it.

6. Then add the stock and raise the heat to high.
7. Combine the fish sauce, saffron (if using), turmeric, and lime juice in a large mixing bowl. Stir all together thoroughly.
8. Allow 15 to 20 minutes for the rice to cook.
9. Remove the lid and fold in the peas, gently stirring the rice as you go.
10. Replace the lid and allow the rice to sit for at least 10 minutes.
11. Remove the cover from the rice and fluff with a fork or chopsticks. Taste and season with a pinch of salt if necessary.
12. Garnish with a sprig of fresh basil.

3.10: Easy Stir-Fried Eggplant

Preparation time: 8 minutes

Cooking time: 10 minutes

Servings: 4

Ingredients

- For the Sauce
- Soy sauce: one and a half tablespoon
- Vegetarian oyster sauce: two tablespoons
- Brown sugar: one teaspoon
- Cornstarch: one teaspoon
- Water: two tablespoons
- For the Eggplant
- Oil: two-three tablespoons (for stir-frying)
- Onion: half (would prefer purple onions)
- Garlic cloves: six (minced, divided)
- Red chilies: one-three
- Chinese Japanese eggplants: one large/two thinner
- Water: ¼ cup (for stir-frying)
- Soy sauce: two tablespoons
- Fresh basil: half cup (divided)
- Peanuts/cashews: ¼ cup (optional) (dry-roasted, chopped)

Instructions:

1. Combine all sauce ingredients, except cornstarch and water, in a mixing bowl.

2. In a separate cup or bowl, combine the cornstarch and water. Set aside.

3. Cut the eggplant into tiny chunks.

4. Over medium-high heat, add 2 to 3 tablespoons of oil to a wok or big frying pan. Then add half of the garlic, onion, chili, and eggplant to a mixing bowl.

5. Add in 2 tablespoons soy sauce and continue frying until the eggplant is soft and the white flesh is almost translucent.

6. Add the rest of the garlic and the sauce until the eggplant is tender.

7. Now add the cornstarch-water mixture. Stir constantly to ensure that the sauce thickens evenly. Remove the pan from the heat.

8. If the dish is not salty enough, add soy sauce or lemon/lime juice if it is too salty.

9. Add 3/4 of the fresh basil and mix briefly to combine.

10. Place on a serving platter and top with the remaining basil and chopped nuts, if desired.

3.11: Vegetarian Thai Tom Yum Soup

Preparation time: 20 minutes

Cooking time: 15 minutes

Servings: 4

Ingredients

- Vegetable stock: five-six cups
- Lemongrass: one-two stalks (minced)
- Whole makrut lime leaves: three
- Red chiles: one-two (sliced)
- Garlic cloves: four (minced)
- Galangal/ginger: one-piece, thumb-size (thinly sliced)
- Mushrooms: one cup (fresh and sliced)
- Baby bok choy: two cups (leaves, chopped)
- Cherry tomatoes: one cup
- Coconut milk: half can (optional)
- Brown sugar: one teaspoon
- Soy sauce: three-four tablespoons
- Lime juice: one tablespoon (fresh)
- Soft tofu: one-two cups (cubed)
- Basil: half cup (fresh, roughly chopped for garnish)
- Cilantro leaves: 1/3 cup (fresh, roughly chopped for garnish)

Instructions:

1. Fill a soup pot with stock.
2. Add the garlic, lime leaves, galangal or ginger, lemongrass, and chili to the pan. Bring the broth to a boil until it is very fragrant.
3. Toss in the mushrooms and cook until they are tender.
4. Add the bok choy and cherry tomatoes.
5. Reduce to low heat and stir in the coconut milk, lime juice, sugar, and soy sauce.
6. Gently stir in the soft tofu. Taste the dish and make any required adjustments.

7. Ladle soup into bowls and top with fresh basil and coriander to eat.

3.12: Vegetable Noodle Soup with Tofu & Lemongrass (Vegan/Gluten-Free)

Preparation time: 10 minutes

Cooking time: 20 minutes

Servings: 8

Ingredients

- Rice noodles: one cup
- Vegetable stock: two quarters
- Lemongrass: half cup
- Fresh ginger: two tablespoons (fresh and minced)
- Carrots: one cup (small dice)
- Broccoli: one cup (small florets)
- Bok Choy: One cup (medium chop)
- Coconut milk: two cups (canned)
- Tofu: 14 ounces/one package (drained and cubed)
- Soy sauce: one cup (reduced sodium)
- Fresh basil: half cup (garnishing)
- Sriracha: four ounces (optional)
- Lime zest: optional

Instructions:

1. Combine stock, carrots, ginger, and lemongrass in a soup pot. Bring to a boil.

2. Add the chopped Bok Choy and broccoli florets to the stock and cook until the vegetables are softened but still vivid in color.

3. Pour in the coconut milk.

4. Add tofu and stir gently.

5. Pour in the soy sauce. Stir until it is well blended.

6. Bring a large pot of water to a boil, turn off the heat and add the noodles to the hot water. Enable noodles to soften for 5-8 minutes. Drain the water and set it aside.

7. Toss 1 cup rice noodles in a bowl with the soup and, if desired, sriracha sauce, lime zest, and fresh basil.

3.13: Thai Pumpkin Coconut Soup

Preparation time: 15 minutes

Cooking time: 15 minutes

Servings: 6

Ingredients
- Unsalted butter: one tablespoon
- Onion: one medium (diced)
- Garlic cloves: four (minced)
- Yellow curry powder: one teaspoon
- Pumpkin purée: two ¼ cups
- Vegetable broth: two and a half cups
- Unsweetened coconut milk: one can (13.5 oz)
- Sour cream: for serving
- Pumpkin seeds: for serving

Instructions:

1. In a medium sauté pan over medium-low heat, melt the butter.

2. Cook, stirring regularly, until the onions are translucent, adding garlic, curry powder, and onions.

3. In a blender, add the mixture, pumpkin purée, and vegetable broth and blend until smooth.

4. In a large stockpot set over medium heat, pour the soup and whisk in the coconut milk.

5. Cook, stirring regularly until the soup is thoroughly warmed.

6. Season with salt and pepper to taste.

7. Divide the soup into bowls and top with sour cream and chopped pumpkin seeds when ready to eat.

3.14: Stir-Fried Greens

Preparation time: 5 minutes

Cooking time: 7 minutes

Servings: 2-3

Ingredients

- Chinese broccoli: one bunch
- Oyster sauce: three tablespoons
- Water: two tablespoons
- Soy sauce: one teaspoon
- Sugar: one teaspoon
- Oil: one tablespoon
- Garlic cloves: three (minced)

Instructions:

1. Rinse the broccoli thoroughly and shake off any excess water.

2. Set aside the stalks, which should cut into 1-inch pieces.

3. Cut the leaves into small pieces.

4. Combine the oyster sauce, soy sauce, water, and sugar in a small cup.

5. Over a high flame, heat a wok or a big skillet. Swirl the oil around.

6. Stir in the garlic for a few seconds.

7. Toss in the stalks and leaves, accompanied by the sauce. Stir and toss the vegetables frequently until the leaves are wilted and the stalks are tender.

3.15: Thai Stir-Fried Spinach with Garlic and Peanuts

Preparation time: 10 minutes

Cooking time: 6 minutes

Servings: 2-4

Ingredients

- Fresh spinach: one large bunch
- Garlic cloves: four (finely chopped)
- Red chili: one (optional)
- Vegetable stock: ¼ cup
- Vegetarian oyster sauce/stir-fry sauce: two tablespoons
- Soy sauce: one and a half tablespoons
- Sherry: one tablespoon
- Brown sugar: one teaspoon
- Sesame oil: one teaspoon
- Red pepper: half (optional, sliced thinly)
- Peanuts or cashews: ¼ cup (roughly chopped, for topping)
- Vegetable oil: two tablespoons

Instructions:

1. Combine stock, sherry, oyster sauce, brown sugar, and soy sauce in a cup. Set aside.
2. Drain spinach after rinsing it.
3. Over medium-high heat, heat a wok or a big frying pan.
4. Swirl in 1 to 2 tablespoons vegetable oil, then add the garlic and chili (if using).
5. Add the red pepper flakes (if using).
6. Stir in the spinach for a few seconds.
7. Stir in the stir-fry sauce until the spinach has cooked down to a dark green color.
8. Remove from the heat and taste to adjust the flavors.
9. Drizzle the sesame oil on top and sprinkle the chopped nuts on top.

3.16: Thai Soyabean in Cabbage Cups Recipe

Preparation time: 10 minutes

Cooking time: 45 minutes

Servings: 4

Ingredients

- Soya bean: one cup
- Onions: ¾ cup (chopped)
- Garlic: two teaspoons (chopped)
- Green chilies: two teaspoons (chopped)
- Tomato sauce: two tablespoons
- Coriander: three tablespoons (chopped)
- Soya sauce: two and a half tablespoons
- Thai red curry paste: one tablespoon
- Bean sprouts: half cup
- Peanuts: optional
- Lemon: ¾ juice
- Spring onion: as desired
- Coriander: chopped
- Chili flakes: as desired

Instructions:

1. Soak the soybean for at least half an hour in water.3-4 times washed. Now squeeze them to remove all of the water.
2. Heat one tablespoon of oil in a wok.
3. Cook the chopped onion in a skillet.
4. Put chopped garlic and green chilies,
5. Add the soya bean. Cook until the water has evaporated.
6. Add the tomato sauce, Thai red curry paste, and soy sauce.

7. Add a pinch of black pepper and continue to cook. Now add the spring onions and cook until they are crisp.
8. Toss in the spring onions, coriander, chili flakes, and a handful of toasted peanuts.
9. Squeeze lemon juice and taste for salt.
10. Serve with small cabbage cups as a garnish.

3.17: Thai-Style Baked Seasoned Sweet Potatoes and Purple Yams

Preparation time: 10 minutes

Cooking time: 50 minutes

Servings: 4-6

Ingredients
- Sweet potatoes: two (peeled and cubed)
- Yams: three-four (purple, peeled, and cubed)
- Large carrot: one (chopped/sliced)
- Coconut oil/vegetable oil: three tablespoons
- Cayenne pepper: half teaspoon
- Cumin: ¼ teaspoon
- Cumin seeds: one teaspoon (whole)
- Syrup: two tablespoons (brown rice/maple syrup)
- Salt: to taste
- Black pepper: to taste
- Coriander: one handful (chopped fresh)
- Red chili: one chopped (optional, for garnish)

Instructions:

1. Preheat the oven to 350 degrees Fahrenheit.
2. In a flat casserole dish, combine the chopped vegetables. Sprinkle the cumin seeds, cayenne pepper, and ground cumin over the oil.
3. To mix, toss all together thoroughly.

4. Place the dish in the oven for 45 minutes after adding three tablespoons of water.
5. Remove the vegetables from the oven when they are tender. Add the butter (if using) and drizzle over the syrup, leaving them in the baking dish. Season with salt and pepper and toss to combine.
6. Taste it and add more salt if necessary.
7. Garnish with coriander and chili (if using).

Chapter 4: Mouthwatering Desserts Recipes

Thai desserts are simply irresistible because they are simple, refreshing, and nutritious.

These desserts will not break your heart if you have a serious sweet craving. They will certainly put you in a good mood!

4.1: Thai Mango Sticky Rice Dessert

Preparation time: 1 hour

Cooking time: 30 minutes

Servings: 6

Ingredients

- Glutinous rice: one and a half cup
- Cups unsweetened coconut milk: one 1/3 cup
- Granulated sugar: half cup
- Salt: ¼ teaspoon
- Sesame seeds: one tablespoon (toasted lightly)
- Large mango: one (diced peeled, and pitted)

Instructions

1. In cold water, soak the rice for 30 minutes.
2. In a big saucepan, combine the rice and 2 cups of water. Put to a boil, covered.
3. Reduce the heat and cook for 15-20 minutes until the water begins to boil.
4. In another pot, add 1 cup coconut milk and 1/4 cup sugar. Cook until the sugar dissolves.
5. Add the mixture slowly over the cooked rice and enable it to sit for 30 minutes. **Prepare the sauce**
6. Cook the remaining sugar and coconut milk in a small saucepan over low heat for around 10-15 minutes.
7. Serve the sticky rice with sliced or cubed mango, drizzled with coconut sauce, and sesame seeds sprinkled on top.

4.2: Musician's Dessert

Preparation time: 15 minutes

Cooking time: 0 minutes

Servings: 4

Ingredients

- Hazelnuts: one handful
- Pine nuts: one handful
- Almonds: one handful
- Walnuts: one handful
- Dried apricots: one handful
- Raisins: one handful
- Dried figs: one handful
- Prunes: one handful

Instructions:

1. Place each handful of fruit or nuts on a serving platter, grouped by type. Enjoy!

4.3: Avocado Cream Dessert

Preparation time: 55 minutes

Cooking time: 0 minutes

Servings: 4

Ingredients:

- Avocadoes: two (large ripe)
- Lime: one (large)
- Tablespoons icing sugar: five tablespoons (sifted)
- Mint leaves: small
- Lime slices: thin

Instructions:

1. Cut the avocados in half lengthwise, remove the stones, and peel them.
2. In a food processor, cut the pulp into small pieces and puree it.
3. To avoid discoloration, combine the puree with some or all of the lime juice and sweeten it with the icing sugar. Stir well.
4. It's better eaten chilled, but not frozen.
5. Garnish with lime slices and mint leaves.

4.4: Thai Dessert Rice Cups

Preparation time: 15 minutes

Cooking time: 25 minutes

Servings: 4

Ingredients
- Coconut milk: one 2/3 cups
- Water: one 1/3 cups
- Short grain rice: one and a half cups
- Sugar: three tablespoons
- Salt: two tablespoons
- Thai mangos: two (ripe)
- White nectarine: three

Instructions:

1. Remove the thick layer of coconut milk from the tin, leaving half of it.
2. Boil liquid coconut milk with water.
3. Stir in the short-grain rice, salt, and sugar.
4. Cook, covered, for 25 minutes over low heat, or until the rice is tender.
5. Now add the coconut cream to the rice.
6. Remove the stones from 5 nectarines halves, wash and halve them. The remaining half should be cut into thin wedges.

7. Cut eight thin wedges from one of the mangoes. Peel and dice the remaining mangoes.
8. Divide the sticky rice among four large glasses, top with diced fruit, and serve with fruit wedges on the side.

4.5: Mini Pudding in Sweet Coconut Sauce

Preparation time: 1 hour

Cooking time: 35 minutes

Servings: 6

Ingredients

- Pineapple: 110g (small cubed)
- Self-raising flour: 125g
- Soft brown sugar: 75g
- Desiccated coconut: 15g
- Egg: 2
- Olive oil: three tablespoons
- Baking powder: half teaspoon
- Ground cinnamon: half teaspoon
- Pineapple juice: 130ml
- Ingredients for Sweet Coconut sauce
- Coconut milk: 100ml
- Sugar: 30g
- Butter: 20g

Instructions:

1. Preheat the oven to 180 degrees Fahrenheit.
2. Soak the desiccated coconut for 1 hour in pineapple juice.
3. In a bowl, whisk together the egg, sugar, and oil with an electric whisk until frothy.
4. In a large bowl, combine flour, soaked desiccated coconut, cinnamon, pineapple, baking powder, and juice. (Do not overmix.)

5. Divide the mixture between the molds. Bakes until it rises to a golden brown color (20-25 minutes).
6. Remove the molds from the oven. Allow it to cool.
7. Make the sauce, melt the butter in a saucepan, then stir in the sugar and coconut milk.
8. Simmer until the sauce thickens.
9. Take the mini cakes out of the molds. Flip it over and drizzle the Sweet Coconut Sauce on top. Stunning!

4.6: Thai- style Pineapple Fritter

Preparation time: 25 minutes

Cooking time: 15 minutes

Servings: 4

Ingredients
- Fresh pineapple: half (or three cups tinned pineapple)
- Tempura flour: one package
- Oil: two cups
- Honey: half tablespoon
- Vanilla ice cream: two and a half cups

Instructions:

1. Peel the pineapple and dice the flesh.
2. Make a batter with the tempura flour as directed on the package.
3. Place the pineapple cubes in the batter, making sure that each one is fully coated.
4. In a wok, heat the oil and deep fry the chunks until golden.
5. Serve the warm pineapple fritters with ice cream and honey in the dishes.

4.7: Thai mango ice cream

Preparation time: 20 minutes

Cooking time: 0 minutes

Servings: 6

Ingredients

- Mangos: two (fresh, ripe)
- White sugar: one cup
- Coconut milk: three tablespoons
- Lemon juice: one teaspoon
- Whipping cream: one cup

Ingredients:

1. Peel and slice the mangoes.
2. In a food processor, place the fruit—Blitz for 1 minute with the sugar.
3. Blitz the coconut milk and lemon juice together for a few seconds to mix.
4. Pour the mango puree into a bowl.
5. Fill the food processor or blender halfway with whipping cream. Blitz the cream until stiff peaks form or it is very stiff.
6. Blitz the mango puree with the whipped cream for 5 to 10 seconds, or until a strong mango-cream consistency is achieved.
7. Fill an ice cream tub with the mixture and freeze for at least 6-8 hours.
8. Scoop into ice cream cones or serve in bowls.

4.8: Thai Banana-Lychee Dessert in Coconut Milk

Preparation time: 5 minutes

Cooking time: 5 minutes

Servings: 2-3

Ingredients
- Ripe bananas: two small
- Coconut milk: one can (regular or light)
- Brown sugar: 1/4-1/3 cup
- Pinch salt: one pinch
- Lychees: eight-ten (fresh or canned)

Instructions:
1. Peel the bananas and cut them into 2-inch slices.
2. In a saucepan, heat the coconut milk over medium heat.
3. Stir in the sugar and salt until they are fully dissolved.
4. Add 1/4 cup sugar. Put a little more if you like it sweeter.
5. Add the bananas and lychees. Stir until the bananas and lychees are thoroughly warmed (1 to 2 minutes).
6. Serve chill or warm.

4.9: Star Fruit in Mango-Orange Sauce

Preparation time: 8 minutes

Cooking time: 10 minutes

Servings: 2-3

Ingredients

- Star fruit: one ripe (fresh, trimmed, seeds removed and sliced)
- Orange juice: one cup
- Mango: one ripe (fresh)
- Brown sugar: ¼ cup
- Coconut milk: one cup
- Pomegranate seeds/cherries: a handful (fresh) (optional)

Instructions:

1. Place the star fruit slices in a pot on the burner.
2. Add the orange juice to the mix. Turn the heat to high and constantly stir until the juice starts to boil.
3. Reduce the heat to low and let the juice simmer for 10 minutes.
4. In a blender, puree the mango. Blend until the mixture is smooth and pureed.
5. When the star fruit is almost done, add the sugar/sweetener and mix to dissolve.
6. Remove the pot from the flame.
7. Stir in the mango puree until it is fully incorporated. Adjust the sugar to your liking.
8. Place 3-star fruit slices per dish with enough sauce to completely cover the fruit.
9. Drizzle some coconut milk on top.

4.10: Thai Sweet Chili and Caramel Topping

Preparation time: 4 minutes

Cooking time: one minute

Servings: 2

Ingredients

- Vanilla ice cream: six scoops
- Fresh mint/basil leaves: garnish
- Peanuts or cashews: crushed or chopped (optional)
- Thai sweet chili caramel sauce:
- Sweet Thai chili sauce: four tablespoons
- Maple syrup: four tablespoons
- Salt: a pinch
- Lime juice: half tablespoon

Instructions:

1. In a saucepan, combine all of the sauce ingredients.
2. Place the saucepan over medium heat and constantly stir for 1 minute.
3. In each serving bowl, put 2 to 3 scoops of vanilla ice cream. Now spoon the warm sauce over the top, dividing it evenly.
4. Serve right away and enjoy.

4.11: Thai Bananas in Coconut Milk

Preparation time: 15 minutes

Cooking time: 5 minutes

Servings: 2

Ingredients

- Bananas: two (peeled, thick rounds slices)
- Coconut milk: 180ml
- White sesame seeds: one and a half tablespoon
- White sugar: 90g
- Water: 120ml
- Salt: half teaspoon

Instructions:

1. Mix sugar and water in a pot over medium heat until sugar dissolves.
2. Cook for 10 minutes after adding the sliced bananas.
3. Take the bananas out of the pot.
4. Add coconut milk, sesame seeds, and 1/2 tsp salt to the same pan.
5. Bring to a boil, then turn off the heat.
6. Over the bananas, drizzle the coconut milk sauce and sprinkle with white sesame seeds. Serve immediately.

4.12: Coconut Tapioca Pudding with Mango and Lime

Preparation time: 10 minutes

Cooking time: 20 minutes

Servings: 6

Ingredients

- Coconut milk: two cans
- Tapioca granules: ¼ cup
- Unsweetened coconut: half cup (shredded)
- Honey: two tablespoons
- Fresh mango: one (peeled and chopped)
- Zest of lime: one
- Extra honey: for drizzling

Instructions:

1. In a saucepan, heat the coconut milk over medium heat until it simmers.
2. Add the tapioca and shredded coconut, cook for 15 minutes, stirring frequently.
3. Combine the honey and place the mixture in the refrigerator to set.
4. Place mango chunks, a drizzle of honey, and lime zest on top of the tapioca pudding in bowls. Have fun!

4.13: Banana Spring Rolls

Preparation time: 10 minutes

Cooking time: 10 minutes

Servings: 8

Ingredients

- Large bananas: two
- Spring roll wrappers: eight (square)
- Brown sugar: one cup
- Oil: for deep frying

Instructions:

1. Preheat the oil in a deep fryer.
2. Bananas should be peeled and cut in half lengthwise.
3. Place one slice of banana diagonally around the corner of a spring roll wrapper and Sprinkle brown sugar to taste.
4. Continue rolling from the corner to the middle, folding the top and bottom corners in as you go. Brush the last edge with your finger dipped in water to seal it. Rep with the rest of the banana slices.
5. Fry a few banana rolls at a time until they are evenly browned in the hot oil. Serve warm or chilled.

4.14: Thai Steamed Banana Cake

Preparation time: 20 minutes

Cooking time: 20 minutes

Servings: 6

Ingredients

- Flaked coconut: one package
- Salt: ¼ teaspoon
- Rice flour: half cup
- Tapioca flour: ¾ cup
- Arrowroot starch: half tablespoon
- Unsweetened coconut cream: one cup
- White sugar: half cup
- Ripe bananas: one pound (mashed)
- Coconut milk: half cup

Instructions:

1. In a cup, combine the coconut and 1/4 teaspoon salt; set aside.
2. In a big mixing bowl, sift together the rice flour, arrowroot starch, and tapioca flour.
3. Mix in the coconut cream and stir for at least 10 minutes.
4. Then add the sugar and stir it in until it dissolves.
5. Mix in the mashed banana thoroughly.
6. Mix in coconut milk and 1/8 teaspoon salt thoroughly.
7. Fill a baking tin (square) or aluminum foil cups with the batter. Garnish with the coconut that was set aside.
8. Bring about 1-1/2 inches of water to a boil in a steamer with a big basket; steam the cake for 20 to 25 minutes over boiling water until it is cooked through.

4.15: Shaved Ice Dessert - Thai Style

Preparation time: 10 minutes

Cooking time: 5 minutes

Servings: 1

Ingredients

- Dried basil seeds: one tablespoon
- Shaved ice: one cup
- Croutons/bread chunky pieces: 10 grams
- Red syrup: three tablespoons
- Condensed milk: one teaspoon (sweetened)

Instructions:

1. Soak dried basil seeds for 30 minutes in 1/2 cup warm water.
2. In a bowl, arrange croutons, soaked basil seeds, and ice to make the dessert.
3. Pour your desired amount of syrup over the ice and drizzle with condensed milk.

4.16: Easy Thai Fruit Salad

Preparation time: 15 minutes

Cooking time: 0 minutes

Servings: 6

Ingredients

- Pineapple cubes: one cup (fresh/canned)
- Banana: one (sliced)
- Mango: one cup (peeled and cubed)
- Lychee fruit: one cup (fresh/canned)
- Star fruit: one (peeled and sliced)
- Strawberries: two cups

- For the dressing:
- Coconut milk: ¼ cup
- Lime juice: one tablespoon (freshly squeezed)
- Sugar: three tablespoons

Instructions:

1. In a cup, whisk together the dressing ingredients until the sugar is dissolved.

2. In a mixing bowl, combine all of the fresh fruit. Toss the fruit with the dressing to thoroughly combine it.

3. In a serving dish, scoop the fruit salad.

4. Garnish with a star fruit slice just before serving.

Chapter 5: Thai Drinks Recipes

Thai drinks with ice are great for quenching your thirst. The following are some Thai drinks that are simple to make at home.

5.1: Lychee-Thai Chili Lemonade Recipe

Preparation time: 15 minutes

Servings: 4-6

Ingredients

- Lychees: one and a half cup (peeled and seeded)
- Fresh juice: one cup
- Sugar: ¾ cup
- Salt: a pinch
- Red Thai chili: half small
- Coldwater: three cups
- Ice: one quart

Instructions:

1. In a blender, combine 1 cup lychees, salt, lemon juice, Thai chili, and sugar.
2. Blend at high speed for 1 minute or until smooth.
3. Strain into a pitcher using a fine-mesh strainer.
4. Mix in the cold water with a whisk.
5. Add the remaining lychee flesh to the pitcher, chopped into 1/4-inch sections.
6. Add ice and serve in ice-filled glasses with whole chilis on top if desired.

5.2: Tom Yum Coca-Cola

Preparation time: 10 minutes

Servings: 1

Ingredients:

- Coca-cola: 200ml
- Lime juice: two teaspoon
- Chopped red chili: ¼ teaspoon (chopped)
- Parsley: two leaf
- Kaffir lime leaf: one (shredded)
- Lemongrass: one stalk
- Salt: one pinch

Instructions:

1. In a tumbler glass, combine the Kaffir lime leaf, parsley, chili, lime juice, salt, and plenty of ice.
2. In a bottle, pour Coca-Cola.
3. Stir all of the ingredients with lemongrass.
4. Serve with a few parsley leaves as a garnish.

5.3: Pandan and Lemongrass Tea

Preparation time: 5 minutes

Cooking time: 5 minutes

Servings: 2

Ingredients

- Lemongrass: six-eight stalks
- Pandan Leaves: for whole
- Sugar: one cup
- Water: two liters

Instructions:

1. Cut the Lemongrass and Pandan leaves into small pieces and boil them in 1 liter of water for about 5 minutes.
2. After removing the herbs, add the sugar and dissolve it completely. Put in the cold water until the tea reaches 2 liters.
3. Enable to cool fully after removing from the heat.
4. Strain the tea through a fine-mesh strainer or a cloth filter.
5. Garnish with fresh lemongrass stalk in the glass and serve over crushed ice.

5.4: Lychee Champagne Cocktail

Preparation time: 5 minutes

Servings: 6

Ingredients

- Lychees syrup: 425g (canned)
- Champagne/sparkling wine

Instructions:

1. Blend 425g canned lychees in syrup until smooth.

2. Freeze until solid in a plastic jar. Pour Champagne or sparkling wine over the frozen lychee in Champagne flutes.

5.5: Thai One On

Preparation time: 10 minutes

Servings: 2

Ingredients
- Thai basil leaves: three
- Sugar: half teaspoon
- Lemongrass-infused vodka: two ounces
- Domaine de Canton: one ounce (ginger liqueur)
- Grapefruit juice: two ounces
- Lemon juice: one teaspoon
- Ice cubes
- Seltzer

Instructions:

1. Combine basil leaves and sugar in a muddle until the basil leaves are thoroughly mashed.
2. Stir the vodka, lemon juice, liqueur, and grapefruit juice.
3. Strain and pour into two glasses.
4. Fill each glass halfway with ice, then top with seltzer. Serve garnished with a sprig of Thai basil or a lemongrass blade.

5.6: Thai Basil Daiquiri Recipe

Preparation time: 3 minutes

Servings: 2

Ingredients

- Thai basil leaves: ten large
- Simple syrup: one and a half ounces
- Lime juice: two ounces
- White rum: four ounces
- Salt: a pinch

Instructions:

1. In a blender, combine all of the ingredients and blend until smooth.
2. Fill a cocktail shaker halfway with ice, then pour in the blended mixture and shake until thoroughly chilled.
3. Strain into two cocktail glasses using a fine-mesh strainer. Serve

5.7: Thai Lemonade

Preparation time: 15 minutes

Servings: 3

Ingredients

- Regular limes: two
- Lemonade concentrate: 2/3 cup (frozen)
- Cold simple syrup: half cup
- Mint leaves: six (fresh)
- Mint sprig: three
- Thai chile: one
- Sea salt: ¼ teaspoon

Instructions:

1. Quarter the limes, cut, and removed the white cores and the seeds.
2. Add 3 cups of ice cubes, mint leaves, sea salt, frozen lemonade concentrate, limes chile, and simple syrup in a blender.
3. Whirl until fully smooth, stirring frequently.
4. Pour into glasses and garnish with a mint sprig. Serve right away.

5.8: Thai-Style Pina Colada

Preparation time: 10 minutes

Servings: 2

Ingredients
- Unsweetened coconut milk: one can
- Pineapple juice: one cup
- Light rum: four ounces
- Sugar: half cup
- Ice cubes: four cups

Instructions:

1. In a blender container, blend the coconut milk, rum, sugar, and pineapple juice.
2. Blend on high until fully smooth.
3. Add ice and blend until it forms a slushy consistency.
4. Pour into the glasses. Serve right away.

5.9: Thai Iced Tea Recipe

Preparation time: 5 minutes

Cooking time: 15 minutes

Servings: 2

Ingredients
- Loose rooibos: two tablespoons
- Boiling water: two cups
- Almond extract: 1/8 teaspoon
- Stevia: twelve drops
- Ice cubes: twenty
- Coconut milk: half cup (full fat)

Instructions:

1. Fill a 2 cup measuring cup with loose tea.
2. Pour hot water over tea; steep for 15 minutes with almond extract and stevia.
3. Fill two large glasses with ice cubes,
4. Strain the tea, and pour it into glasses.
5. Add the coconut milk and serve.

5.10: Thai Lemon Iced Tea

Preparation time: 5 minutes

Servings: 1

Ingredients

- Thai tea mix: one teaspoon
- Boiled water; one cup
- Lime juice: 2 teaspoons
- Raw honey: 2 teaspoons
- Ice cubes
- Sliced lime: for garnish

Instructions:

1. Steep the Thai tea mix for a few minutes in boiling water and strain.
2. Add the lime juice and honey.
3. Taste and make adjustments based on personal preference.
4. Fill a tall glass with ice and pour in the Thai lemon tea.
5. Serve with lime slices on top.

Conclusion

Vegan and vegetarian eating is becoming more common in Thailand, and these dishes demonstrate how delicious vegan Thai cuisine can be. Many of the recipes are also gluten-free so that no one would be left out. These recipes are full of Thai flavor and are also well-balanced in terms of nutrition.

After reading this book, you will discover that preparing your favorite Thai vegetarian dishes at home is easy. In this book, the different ingredients used in vegetarian Thai recipes are also discussed. There are 70 recipes in this cookbook, including breakfast, lunch, dinner, desserts, and a few drinks. These recipes are simple to prepare at home and do not require any supervision.

So, get cooking today and enjoy your delectable Thai vegetarian cuisine.

Printed in Great Britain
by Amazon